# From Russia To Wales

*With Love*

MARINA STORINA

Balboa Press books may be ordered through booksellers or by contacting:

Balboa Press
A Division of Hay House
1663 Liberty Drive
Bloomington, IN 47403
www.balboapress.co.uk
UK TFN: 0800 0148647 (Toll Free inside the UK)
UK Local: 02036 956325 (+44 20 3695 6325 from outside the UK)

ISBN: 978-1-9822-8653-8 (sc)
ISBN: 978-1-9822-8652-1 (e)

Print information available on the last page.

Balboa Press rev. date: 10/26/2022

A DIVISION OF HAY HOUSE

# From Russia to Wales

*With Love*

# From Russia to Wales

WITH LOVE

MARINA STORINA

# CONTENTS

# FOREWORD

*'I will carry the light of love for you my family as an eternal cross of salvation in my soul.'*
— Marina Storina, from the poem *'To my family and country'*.

In the same way that no two snowflakes are the same, although we are all part of one universal web, we are uniquely different.

We are all born as beautiful babies with a strong desire to tell our personal story through our life experiences on this Earth.

Our journey begins with the connection to our place of birth. Without realising it, we all carry on our family legacy by sharing our DNA story with each other on the incredible planet that we call home.

This book is my story of how the events that have unfolded in my life have led me to an understanding of the gifts that I have been given by the generations that came before.

In sharing my family story, I want to pay a huge thanks

to those whose story has already ended. It's an appreciation of members of my family, and yours, who lived their lives before us, preparing us to explore the opportunities that came our way so we could do the same for our own children.

Reflecting on my life, I can now see clearly who I am, where I came from and where I am going. My journey started in Russia in 1966, was followed by my experiences in Germany in the 1980s and led to my unexpected move to Wales in 1998, through some extraordinary life events that often involved confronting my fears. It was only once I learned to 'own' my fears that I started to see my journey in life become real and profound.

Looking back, I have realised that my fears are the most treasured gifts that I possess and that they blessed me with a love for what I do professionally. After so many setbacks along the way, I began to ask myself, 'What are you afraid of?'

I found all my fears hidden in boxes named 'what I don't want', 'what I hate' or 'who I hate'. I learned that the people I once hated or frightening events that nearly cost me my life were actually the most important forces in my life, and an overwhelming desire to change my life clearly presented itself.

I finally realised that passing through life carrying this baggage on my back was a miserable exercise, and it was time to cast it aside. Understanding that it was OK to be different gave me permission to drive my own life rather than allowing it to be driven by others.

One by one, my fears were replaced by a desire to love life – not just any sort of life, but a great life full of interest in my own evolution and geared towards the benefit of others, helping people to stay healthy and happy.

That force became unstoppable and has kept me going, regardless of life's challenges – transforming people's lives through my business and serving the community that I have called home for over 24 years.

I know now that I was born to love and shine that energy towards everyone I meet, regardless of what they think of me. That knowledge came with the realisation that profoundly deaf people feel OK to be deaf with a capital D.

In practical terms, our ears provide us with our sense of hearing. As an audiologist with 18 years' experience, I should know! But there's more to it than that. I have also discovered that the function of hearing provides us with an amazing sense of wellbeing about ourselves and the world around us. We feel good when we hear about good things or good events, and we are miserable when we hear negative things about ourselves or others.

I have learned from my patients that, despite our hearing ability or absence of it, we can all 'hear' with our intuition. It's a gift we all possess but listening to that intuition is a skill and requires constant practice.

People who are born deaf navigate their path through life with 'gut feelings', or feelings in their hearts, far more skilfully than others. Perhaps this is because they grow up listening to their inner voice rather than hearing all the negativity others direct towards them – and this leads to them feeling good about being different.

My dream is that people on their personal journey through life will come to realise, as I have, that loving ourselves for our differences is not a selfish act but a divine state of being that it is our birthright, helping us to communicate with our intuitive self.

This book is not going to tell you what to do. It's just my story of how I have learned to listen to my fears using my intuition and turn them into a message of love, giving me the ability to choose whether to be a victim or a winner.

It's a story of my soul journey from Russia to Wales with love.

# 1

## LETTER FROM THE FRONT

My family name, Storin/a, came from my granddad, who was born in the north of Russia and successfully completed infantry school training in 1939 at an academy just outside Moscow. This was where he met my grandmother Galina, who was working there as a secretory.

In spring 1944, battle was raging in Crimea, where the Red Army were trying to push back the occupying German forces. My grandfather was one of the officers fighting on the front line.

The death toll on both sides was high, and there was no end to the war in sight. Russia was on its knees, and my grandfather and his comrades were painfully aware of the hardships their families had been facing back home.

Despite the situation in Crimea, he somehow found the time to write regularly to my grandmother, who was living in Moscow with their two small boys. They were lovely, comforting letters showing no fear or emotion. Thankfully, by this stage, some supplies were finally entering the city.

In one of those letters, he wrote:

*My dear Galina,*

*It is so nice to see your picture. It arrived so late. Now it's spring, and your picture is of you in a warm scarf and old coat. So sorry you were so cold in the winter and I couldn't be there with you. Your old coat and the big scarf around your neck make you look even thinner. I know, my dear, it was a very hard winter for you and my two little boys – my Slavik and my newborn, Yuri.*

*I am very sorry that my first boy has been so ill and can hardly stand on his own two feet. I am sure you care for him and are doing your best, but please remember you need to eat too. I am sending you all my allowances because I can manage with the soldiers here. There is plenty of bread, although it's not the kind of bread my ma used to make of course! But it will do. We all must to stick together and push through.*

*The other day, we had a battle, and it was so bloody. I lost any sense of who was on our side and who was the enemy. You can't really identify people by their uniforms anymore because they haven't been washed or pressed. Everyone is dirty, just one big mess.*

*You can't see the water of the Black Sea, there is so much blood – and bodies everywhere. It's scary.*

*God, I hope this will be over soon and we can return to some sort of normality.*

*During the fighting, I came face-to-face with a young German soldier. I am a strong, tall man, but that little German boy was so frightened. He was probably 14 or 15, very thin – and I was expected to kill him in this battle? Sorry, but I couldn't do that. I thought about my boys. He is somebody's son, and what if his mother receives the terrible news that he has been killed? At least I have two boys already, but that boy didn't even have a chance to experience a woman's kiss or a woman's body or just friendship. He had never even shaved. He had a little fluff around his upper lip, and he was very scared. His blue eyes became icy cold when I came up towards him, and I just said to him, 'Shoosh, run, run, run quickly and hide. You must . . .'*

*That's it. Not much to tell. Every day becomes the same. Blood, fear, bread to share. Another day, I gave my soldiers something to eat because, as officers, we receive much more than them. I am very sad, and I am hoping I will see you and my boys soon.*

*All my love to you and to my beautiful boys.*
*Yours always,*
*Nicolai.[1]*

---

[1] Nicolai Storin, who was Captain-commander of the 915th Battery of the Artillery Regiment 345th Division was killed in action defending his home, family and freedom in the port of Sebastopol, Crimea on 20th April 1944. He was decorated as a war hero. I proudly named my son Nick after him as a reminder of where I came from and what price my granddad paid for my existence.

# 2

## MY GRANDMA GALINA

My father's mother Galina Storina was openly religious and a devoted churchgoer. Yet she was a modern lady who had been widowed when my grandfather Captain-commander Nicolai Storin was killed as a hero in 1944 fighting in the Second World War.

Born in 1913, she grew up to be a stunning looking woman with a lovely figure and an eye for fashion. She was very good at sewing and, as an army officer's widow, was provided with the materials to make her own clothes. She would take the patterns to a shop and have the cloth cut the way she wanted, then get busy on her sewing machine at home.

Her clothes were immaculate. She used to wear a beautiful pencil skirt with silk tights and white shoes in summer because, even though it was so hot in Moscow, she felt you had to put up with certain things to look your best! My love for clothes, as well as my love for dressing smartly, perhaps came from her.

She never wore jewellery, except the earrings that my grandfather had bought for her, which she never took off. She wore bright lipstick, and I remember her hair was always neatly permed. As a little girl, I would often find her red lipstick in the dresser and try it on, seeing her face smiling at me in the reflection of the mirror.

After Nicolai was killed, she brought up their two boys, my father and uncle, on her own. My dad had been the lucky one of twins. His sister sadly died at birth. Both boys became successful people who were degree-educated and had nice families and homes.

As the widow of a war hero, she was offered a secure office job by the government and worked as a secretary, supporting herself financially. She had also been provided with brand-new accommodation by the state, and in 1966, I was born in that flat. It was modern for the time, with big windows, a telephone on the wall, a TV and a fridge with a rather strange handle!

But there were two very different sides to Grandma Galina. She would go to work in that smart pencil skirt, silk tights and bright lipstick, yet every evening, she would go to church wearing a simple white scarf, flat shoes and a long coat that was old and heavy, like a trench coat. She would stay there for hours and hours.

I remember there were icons in her flat of St Nicholas and a big picture of Jesus Christ on the Cross in her bedroom, despite the fact that in the '60s and '70s, not many people displayed such things.

During the revolution and the Stalin era, many churches had been destroyed and others closed, with priests arrested and sent to the gulags! But it didn't stop her going to church every evening and reading the Bible, which she had given a special cover, as if she didn't want anything to spoil it.

Nowadays in Russia, you can buy a Bible anywhere, but then, it was probably difficult, and being a widow of a hero, she didn't want to fall out with the government. She remembered the Stalin era and people being taken from their own homes without anyone knowing where they had gone. It must have been a dreadful time. I appreciate now that the Bible and church meant a lot to her.

One day, I asked if I could go to church with her, and she said, 'OK.' My mum and dad didn't like this idea, using the excuse that church was for older people. I didn't want to get her into trouble, so our visits to church became our 'big secret'.

Because my grandfather's name was Nicolai, she always went to St Nicholas Church, where she would light a big candle for him. I remember going to church with her on a Sunday. Russian Orthodox is derived from Greek Orthodox, a Byzantian religion. I had to wear a scarf and bow to the altar, where the priest gave me a piece of bread and crossed my forehead with holy water and oil. It was beautiful. In the Russian church, you don't sit – you either stand or pray on your knees, like she did.

I also asked Grandma if she would read to me from 'The Book'. At night time, she would treat me to passages from her Bible. I had no idea what the words meant – it was very difficult to understand for a little girl – but when she was reading it, there was an amazing transformation in her. She would light a candle and create a magical environment in her bedroom. It was so peaceful that I would fall asleep and wake up the next morning in my own bed in a different room.

Throughout my life, until quite recently, I didn't understand why my mum and grandma didn't get on. I felt there was some sort of secret that they were never going to share with me. On many occasions, I even asked my parents if I was adopted. It was only last year that I discovered what that secret was. My uncle told me that I have a half-brother, who is a year younger than me, and that no one in my family had the heart to tell me about him.

It's what adults do to children – teach them to pick sides and create secrets, judging people as good or bad. But we are all born as lovely babies with open hearts to love and be loved by others – we just forget about it when we become adults. I am hoping that my mum and my grandma Galina, who are both gone now, settled their differences and their souls are resting free from pain.

But despite the problems between them, I used to love my special time with Grandma Galina. She wrote little poems, and we would laugh as we created stories together. I would often ask my dad if I could stay over with her. From my grandmother's stories, I knew that my grandfather was a good man. I loved to listen to her voice when she read his letters to me. She told me that he was the only one for her. His family wasn't happy for them to be married because she was five years older than him but that he refused to listen.

Although she was a stunning looking woman, I never saw her with another man. No one could imagine her with anyone else. Her heart belonged to her Nicolai, the handsome man who was always smiling in the big photograph of him in military uniform, which she proudly displayed on her bedside table. I know now that my belief in a power bigger than us started with her. That power helped her through terrible times during the war, facing all the hardships with two little children, losing one of her twins at birth, her husband away fighting at the front and then being made a widow at 31.

It was only after being prevented from attending the funerals of both my parents, fearing for my son's life when he was fighting with the British army in Afghanistan and becoming a widow myself at 46 that I was able to understand why her blue eyes never cried, as if there was nothing more to cry about! She never talked about it, but I feel, now more than ever, that her strength came from surrendering all her problems to a much higher power. She just put her head down and got on with life, despite the problems, because sometimes, life's not meant to be understood – it's meant to be accepted.

My grandma Galina died peacefully in 1999 with the Bible in her hands and the photo of my forever young grandfather next to her.

# 3

## THE POWER OF LOVE

My mother's parents were very happy, friendly people. I never heard them argue.

My grandfather Feodor never swore and never drank alcohol. My grandmother Valentina was a strong character who dedicated her life to her family and her local community. Many people came to her flat for advice on all sorts of things – cooking, gardening, growing flowers, knitting and sewing. My kind-hearted, blonde, tall, blue-eyed grandad called her 'The Boss'. Their story was incredible.

On a typically wet and cold day in Leningrad, now St Petersburg, Feodor visited the cinema to watch one of the first USSR films *Battleship Potemkin*. In post-revolution days, Soviet cinematography was the most important of all the arts. He was 26 and far from his family home at the time of the Soviet–Finnish War in 1939–1940, based on the border just outside Leningrad. He was the chauffeur for an army officer, who must have felt sorry for him and allowed him to go to the movies while he was visiting his own family.

Sitting next to him in the cinema that day was my grandma Valentina, who was 23 years old and a student at the vocational school, training to become an army uniform sewing operator. Her dad had brought his family to Leningrad from their family home just outside Moscow – Valentina, her older sister, two brothers aged 17 and 20 and her mum. 1939–1941 was the period of the restoration of the economy and industrialisation. Valentina's dad was one of thousands of industrial labour recruits involved in the government plan to increase vocational training and productivity in Leningrad.

From that day, Feodor started to visit Valentina's family on Nevsky Prospekt, just on the corner near the Aurora cinema where they met. They lived in one of the communal apartments where the family of seven shared one room in a 12-roomed flat. All the amenities – latrines, plumbing, sewerage, stoves, heating and boilers – were shared with the other 11 families.

It was a system introduced after the revolution in 1917, when the new Soviet government came up with the idea of placing the working class in large, multi-roomed apartments that prior to the revolution had been occupied by the middle class. I'm afraid to even imagine what happened to the original owners of these properties.

After the Soviet–Finnish war was over and he was refused the opportunity to progress with his training and become a naval officer based at Red Banner Leningrad Naval Base, Feodor went back to a place near his homeland, the small town of Rybnoy, which is 177 kilometres from Moscow. This meant that he and Valentina were separated by 991 kilometres, which was a 15-hour train journey. Although he tried several times to reapply for naval training, the decision came back the same – refusal on the grounds that he came from a wealthy family.

Feodor's granddad Moses was the owner of several mills and therefore regarded as 'an enemy of the Soviet state'. Moses was lucky to have died in 1916 and not seen everything that he had worked for over the years destroyed. His mills and his large house were burned to the ground, while his wife, his son and his eldest grandson, Feodor's 14-year-old brother, were all shot as enemies of the state in 1918. Only his son's wife and my grandad, aged four, were able to escape.

Feodor never knew his real date of birth, as his mum died of tuberculosis a year after these devastating events. The village church was also burned down by the Soviet state, together with the register of Feodor's birth. All he and his 15-year-old aunt Eudokia knew was that he was born in 1914.

After his mother died, Eudokia looked after him as her own child, and she stayed single all her life. She registered his birthday as 12th February because February and Feodor both began with the letter 'F'! She worked in a hospital during the Second World War, then became a servant of the church and dressed all her life as a nun. My grandad was close to her until her death in 1975, and I remember her as a very old lady that he called 'Dunya', short for Eudokia.

From the age of seven, Feodor became independent and entered factory school in Rybnoye, which was 10 kilometres away from his grandad's family lands and mills. My mum and I only found out about it from his diaries after his death. He never told us much about his family, only that they were all dead. After his death, together with my mum, I went to our family land, which was a wasteland with an old, overgrown cemetery by then. We found the black granite stone bearing the name of Moses Vasilyeva, painted across with the words, 'enemy of the state'.

Valentina was keen to marry Feodor, and her mum and siblings were given the task of arranging the wedding. Her dad stayed behind in Leningrad, planning to follow his family back to their home near Moscow for the wedding, which was planned for 22nd June 1941. When the wedding day arrived, Valentina woke up Feodor, who was sleeping outside the house, and told him that war between Russia and Hitler had been declared at 4 a.m.!

Stalin himself ordered all men of 18 and over to register for service on the Western front. Feodor was sent to the place where he was based during the Soviet–Finnish war, just outside Leningrad, and Valentina followed him. The factory where Valentine 's dad, Ian, was working switched to making equipment needed for the military, and he also had to leave his family.

With Hitler progressing fast, the bombs started falling on Leningrad. Fortunately, Valentina had managed to escape the blockade, but her dad, Ian, died from famine there together with her older brother. The family couldn't even retrieve their bodies for burial.

My mum, Zoya, was born in August 1942. Her parents, however, didn't become husband and wife until 1946 when, to the utter amazement of her mother and others, Feodor, who had been reported missing in action in 1943, came home. To the last day of my granddad's life, my mum was his pride and joy.

My mum adored him too but told me that for a very long time after he returned she was afraid of him because she had only ever seen women's faces around her since she was born. She probably wasn't the only child that felt that way. In the village where she grew up, just one disabled man had been left in charge of 100 women working in the fields providing food for the Red Army.

Sadly her birthplace, home to many families before the war, was flattened by bombs and only 30 women and four children survived.

The war may have changed Feodor and Valentina's plans but it was destined that they would go through everything designed to tear them apart and emerge even stronger. After my grandma Valentina's death in December 1994, my grandad Feodor told us that he was going to see her soon. He left this world in December 1995 with no health problems. He had gone to pick up food for his beloved cat and died outside the door of his flat. Prior to that, he had phoned my house looking for my mum, and his last words to her were that he loved her very much.

# 4

## CHILDHOOD MEMORIES

My grandparents Feodor and Valentina had a nice flat but also a country house not far away. I suppose this 'growing patch' was like an allotment in Britain, but you could also put a small house on it, although you were not allowed to stay there in winter, only in the summer. During the summer months, my other grandma Galina would also stay in their country house for weekends, and the four of us had endless fun.

My favourite fruits have always been tomatoes because my grandmother Valentina was a master tomato grower. Tomatoes were her babies. They were huge, the size of a dog's head. I remember going to market to buy the seeds. The sellers came from all over the place – some from Georgia, some from Azerbaijan, some from Ukraine – and she would grow the seeds in little pots on the windowsill in spring, then transfer them to the greenhouse by the end of April. They had a kind of split border in their vegetable patch, with a greenhouse on her side for her tomatoes. On the other side, my grandfather grew cucumbers, and there was healthy competition between them.

The weather in Russia is very different to Wales. One day in May will be very hot, but there'll be a winter blizzard the next, without any warning. The sudden change would send my parents and grandma Galina to shelter indoors while my grandad Feodor and my dad were frantically searching for something to protect the little tomato plants that Valentina had just transferred to the greenhouse. I remember she'd keep saying, 'Come on, my little babies!'

Staying with my grandparents was my happiest time - waking up in the morning to the smell of one of my grandmother Valentina's delicious omelettes, enjoying a morning workout with my grandad, being in the company of two people who loved each other and everyone around them. The kettle would never get cold because members of the local community kept arriving, borrowing a book from my grandad or seeking some advice from my grandma.

On many occasions, when my parents had had an argument, Grandma Valentina and Grandad Feodor would arrive at our home with nice food, fresh cake and the family's favourite game of bingo to smooth things over. It wasn't surprising to me that my family crumbled after both were gone. For Feodor and Valentina, the priority was love, family and peace, and they were truly grateful for every day they spent together.

Grandad Feodor, who had survived two wars, was always very tearful when he saw the Red Square parade on 9th May, with soldiers marching and veterans looking on. He always put medals on his jacket that day. He also put a shot of vodka with a piece of bread on the dinner table, but it was never touched. I knew he never drank, so I asked him what it was for, and he said it was in memory of all, including my granddad Nicolai, who gave their lives for our future happiness.

When I was little, grandad Feodor used to make up bedtime stories for me, usually with happy endings. If you asked him the next night to continue the story, he'd forgotten what it was about! He also had a good collection of books. Only after his death did I realise how much he loved reading and writing. He would take a minute or two each day to relate in his diary what was happening in the lives of his family and in the world around him. I'm sure he couldn't imagine turning these diary entries into books, but if he had, he would have made us proud.

The love that my grandparents shared for each other was contagious, as if a magnet attracted people towards them, including me. My mum's mother, Valentina, taught me all sorts of practical things – sewing, cooking, making bread, caring for the house – not that my mum was bad at that, but she never had the time.

My grandmother also inspired my love of flowers. She used to bring us flowers as gifts, and occasionally, she took them to market. She had this commercial gene in her that she passed on to me. Whatever she produced, she liked to sell, and what she couldn't sell, she would give away.

She valued her financial independence. I know that after the Second World War, she worked as a bookkeeper in an adult evening school. She had never used her qualifications as a military uniform sewing operator, but she was exceptional at maths. Though she had to give up her job after she had a serious heart attack. It was one of the most frightening events in my childhood. I remember we flew back to Moscow from our summer holiday in Georgia and rushed to the hospital, where I saw my grandad sobbing. I asked him if my grandma Valentina was dead, and he said no, but she was very poorly.

When I went to my room that night, I decided to copy the people I'd seen in church with my grandma Galina. I just wasn't ready to lose my grandmother, so I fell to my knees and was crossing myself and putting my forehead to the floor in the hope she would live to grow tomatoes and make strawberry jam again, that we would sew and knit together, and my grandad would drive us to country house through the forest, both laughing.

When I woke very early the next morning, the telephone was ringing, and I heard my dad speaking to someone. My heart was pounding in my ears, but somehow, I felt it was good news, that whatever I had wished for had been granted. A few minutes later, my father came into my room, smiling and said, 'Do you want to see your grandma Valentina?' I remember the joy.

At the hospital, they gave me a white coat to wear that was so long it almost reached the floor. We went in, and my grandma was lying there flat on her back with no pillows. The nurse said, 'You mustn't talk to her – do you understand?' I asked if she was alive, and a doctor came up and said, 'Of course she is. You can touch her hand if you want to.' So I touched her hand. Her eyes were closed, and her hand was very sweaty. She couldn't speak, but I could feel her hand squeeze my finger, like she was saying, 'Hello'. From that day on, she started to get better and lived on for many happy years.

The thought of my grandmother and her flowers has always remained in my heart. She particularly loved peonies. She had beautiful bushes of them in white and pink and used to bring them to us as a present with a little note saying, 'From Valentina to my girls', meaning Mum and me. Today, I bought peony perfume because I wanted a little reminder of her and my happy childhood with both of my grandparents.

# 5

## MY WONDERFUL PARENTS

A child without parents becomes an orphan. Although I am no longer a child, as time has passed since I lost my mum and dad, I have been feeling more and more like an orphan myself. I bow to both of them with respect and gratitude for bringing me into this world and providing me with a safe, healthy and happy childhood.

Ironically, my mum started off by dating my dad's brother, so the chance of my existing at all is a miracle in itself! As a toddler, my dad survived tuberculosis, which left his lungs permanently scarred. As a result, he failed his medical and was unable to study with his brother at the Secondary Military Educational Institute, named after the Russian commander A.V. Suvorov, in Moscow. Instead, he joined the navy and later successfully completed his studies at Moscow Engineering Physics Institute, becoming a deputy director responsible for managing the operations of the plant, with thousands of employees.

When I was a teenager, I tried to out-smart him by telling him that I had done my homework and completed my hourlong piano practice so that I could go skating with my school friends. But he didn't fall for my white lie and explained that my school work and my musical practice were really important, and I must always do my work to the best of my ability and with pride. He was true to his word, getting up every morning at 5 a.m., pressing his trousers and shirt and polishing his shoes ready to start work at 8 a.m. His aim was always 'to do your best all day and every day'.

When I was six years old, my parents signed me up for swimming classes. Unfortunately, my first lesson was a disaster. We were told to put our faces under the water, and all the kids around me were doing it with no problem. But I couldn't understand how I could breathe like that, and I refused to do it and left the pool. I still remember the look on my mum's face when I appeared in the foyer wearing only my swimming gear and standing bare foot on the freezing floor in front of her.

On the way home, she lectured me about my behaviour. At home, my dad listened to my explanation and promised that he would teach me to swim during our next holiday to the Black Sea. With his help, I became a strong swimmer and was never again afraid of holding my breath underwater! The lesson I learned from my dad was to always use logic when dealing with your fears. Having instilled this attitude in me, he also taught me how to ride a bike and how to dance on ice.

He never allowed me to argue with my mum, who was both talented and a strong leader in her own right. After graduating from her first university in 1964, she taught German there. Then, in 1987, she completed another degree at the University of Patris Lumumba in Moscow and became head of the Russian language department for foreign students at the Higher School of the Ministry of Internal Affairs (police academy), as well as chairperson of the trade union committee.

I only truly understood what an important person my mum was when two busloads of her students and colleagues from the academy and the union committee turned up at her funeral and a memorial was unveiled in her honour at her university. Unfortunately, due to COVID-19 restrictions, I was only able to follow her funeral via Zoom. My dad died very suddenly, and again, I couldn't make it to his funeral due to a bureaucratic delay with my passport, which had gone missing during my application for permanent residency in the UK.

Struggling with their deaths and being unable to attend both of their funerals, I wrote last year: 'I will carry the light of love for you, my family, as an eternal cross of salvation in my soul'. I am hoping this year to complete a stone monument to all the members of my family who are gone but whose spirit will be with me until my last day.

# 6

## FIRST DAY AT SCHOOL

In one of my grandfather Feodor's diaries he had written: 'Marina went to school. She had a struggle today because she broke her flowers and was really upset'. It reminded me what had happened.

On your first day at school, it was traditional to take in flowers and give them to your teacher as a symbol of your transition from early childhood into education. Mine had come from my grandparents' country house, and they were so big the stems got snapped in the lift on the way. A solution was needed quickly. My grandma Galina started wiping away my tears, and my grandma Valentina said, 'Don't worry! We'll fix it!' and made me a fantastic, state-of-the-art bouquet.

When we walked towards the school, there were a lot of people about. My grandparents and parents were there with me, and I was firmly holding my dad and grandad Feodor's hands because I didn't want to go in, but they said, 'Come on! Go, go!'. As I walked away from them and turned around, they were all there standing in a row, waving.

The day I was leaving Russia in 1998 felt like that first day at school. When I walked towards the plane, fearing that step into the unknown, I turned around, but no one was there to wave to me. I just had my little boy, Nick, walking next to me with a happy smile, holding my hand. Swallowing my tears, I imagined how nice it would have been if all of them had been standing in the airport behind me, saying, 'Come on! Go, go!' But there was no one.

# 7

## SUMMER CAMP

So many things in our lives happen for a reason.

During the school holidays when I was a kid, I used to go to summer and winter camp. In those days, families could buy relatively cheap tickets for these camps via their unions at work. They were great for children aged between seven and 14 because they were based in the forests outside Moscow with amazing sports facilities. They were a bit like scout camps in the UK perhaps, but on a grander scale. They were run by teachers or students on teaching practice from colleges, with cooking and medical facilities on site and security guards at the gates.

The city is very hot in summer, and children break off school for nearly three months at the end of May, unless they are doing exams. It's preferable to escape from the city if you can because the heat is so uncomfortable. In those days, children had to be looked after by the community while their parents worked. They couldn't be running around the streets like now – everything had to be organised.

I was a very competitive child and loved taking part in the sporting activities at the camps, such as swimming in summer and skiing and skating in winter. I also enjoyed meeting children from schools all over Moscow and sometimes outside. Groups of the same age slept in rooms with six beds, with girls, of course, separate from boys. You were all expected to help with the cleaning and preparation of food, such as peeling potatoes.

The activities were not like lessons in school; they were more creative, and there were competitions for different age groups. One of my favourite activities was making a sculpture from wet sand and painting it. I also enjoyed the afternoon discos. Sunday was open day, when parents could come and visit, bringing you fruit, sweets and fresh clothes.

My parents were very organised about what I did in my summer holidays. I used to spend the first month helping my mum's parents, then spend July in camp before going on holiday with my parents in August. In my early childhood, it was Georgia, later Crimea and the Baltic countries.

Although I had a great time at my first summer camp holiday, the second wasn't so good. The weather was unseasonably rainy, and I suffered from home sickness. When my grandad Feodor, grandmas Valentina and Galina and my parents came visit me on the first weekend, I asked them to take me home because I was feeling bored and lonely. My parents refused point blank, saying that I needed to find activities that were not going to be affected by rainy days!

Knowing my grandad Feodor had a kind heart, I started talking to him about what a miserable time I was having because I couldn't do my normal sporting activities and couldn't 'connect' with the other kids because they were all playing table tennis, which I wasn't very good at. When my parents told me the car was full and there was no room for me, my quick response was, 'I'm happy to have a ride in the trunk instead!' They all left anyway, and feeling near to tears, I remained in the camp.

To my surprise, next morning just after breakfast, when I had already forgotten about all this, I saw my grandad Feodor with my ready-packed suitcase in his hand waiting for me outside. When I asked him how he had managed to overturn my parents' ban on me going home, he smiled and told me that the night before, the family had taken a vote, with my grandparents' three votes beating my parents' two, and that was my ticket to freedom. It was the only time I ran away from summer camp.

Ironically, it was at camp, when I was just 11, that I met the boy who was to become my first husband. Looking back, nothing in life is for nothing – meeting him was not an accident. But back then, when we finished camp, we simply exchanged addresses and went our separate ways. Moscow is a big city, and it wasn't possible to meet up with the friends you'd made at camp, but we used to write to each other. It was nice to meet children my own age, and sometimes older, who shared my interests.

I didn't fall for Oleg at that stage of course, but I'm sure I had a picture of him from those days. We used to dance together at the discos in the evening, and we enjoyed each other's company and the same sporting activities. Then, when I was 17, he called me out of the blue at New Year, and after that, we started dating. We eventually got married when I was 18 and he was 19. We were together 12 years, including living for seven years in Germany and having our lovely boy.

Because table tennis had once made me run away from camp, I tried my best to avoid playing it, although both my parents had played competitively at their universities and were really good. I remember when I was a little girl, there were table tennis tables outside our block of flats where the residents, like my parents, could go and play.

Ironically, many years later in the UK, my second husband, David, encouraged me to play again, and much as I tried to avoid it, remembering my poor attempts as a child, I ended up achieving quite good results. I am sure my parents would be very pleased to know that! Interestingly, it was through playing table tennis that I met my now boyfriend, Neil.

*My granddad Storin on the left*

*My grandma (standing) and her sister*

*My dad and grandma Galina*

*My grandma Galina with her mum, older sister and sister's little boy*

*My dad's family, Mr and Mrs Storin. My dad on the right and his little brother on the left.*

*Feodor Leningrad*

баня тоже близко. Есть Столовая для семей нач. в нашем доме.

Отрицательные — плохой ДКА. а в город не находишься и не наездишься, а в особенно нам. Если бы мы ... Но это можно пережить.

Галочка! Я не получил еще за отпуск и зарплату.

Милая Галочка! В квартиру вошел и сейчас ее занимаю.

Признаться, милочка моя, она, конечно по виду уже недойдет до нашей т-е в которой ты живешь, неммотко. Вообщем тебе здесь будет простор. Сама будешь хозяйка. Дрова завозить. Ты только Галочка не пробовай ваночку, ведро и таз, а кровать, комод, матрацы и закрытый курортный столик обязательно пробовай. Слойную кроватку тоже не трожь. Когда куплю, то я напишу, чтобы ты ...

*Letter from my grandfather*

Здравствуйте, дорогой

К Вам обращается сын погибшего капитана СТОРИНА НИКОЛАЯ ТРОФИМОВИЧА.

Мой отец, Николай Трофимович, родился в 1918 году в селе Михайловке Крупецкого района Курской области, окончил сельхозтехникум в Рыльске, а в 1939 году – Рязанское пехотное училище им. Ворошилова. После окончания училища был оставлен на педогогическую работу. В конце 1940 года переведен во Вторую Высшую школу штурманов г.Иванова, затем в Тульское артучилище.

1942 г. – полевая почта №1575 часть 64

1943 г. –     -"-              -"-

1944 г. –     -"-         №18911 часть 13

Последнее место службы – 915 артполк, 346 дивизия, 51 Армия.

Погиб 20 апреля 1944 года северо-западнее 9 км г.Севастополя (при освобождении). В настоящее время числится в списках братской могилы села Холмовка (в 1,5 км от села Фронтовое г.Севастополя).

Убедительная просьба сообщить все, даже самое незначительное, что Вам, а может быть Вашим сослуживцам известно о моем отце.

В последнем письме он сообщил о представлении к званию майора и ордену Александр Невский.

К сожалению иной информацией мы (семья Сториных) не располагаем.

Извините за беспокойство.

к-т Стори Николай Т.ф. 20/IV-44г. – 915 ап п.

Копия

346 дав.

51 армия

И З В Е Щ Е Н И Е

Ваш   Муж Капитан СТОРИН Николай Трофимович уроженец гор.Вологда, Калинная дом 36 в бою за Социалистическую Родину, верной воинской присяги, проявив геройство и мужество  был убит 20.4.44 года  в районе Северо-Западнее 9 килом. г.Севастополь, Крымская АССР. Похоронен брадское кладбище. Настоящее извещение является документом для возбуждения  ходатайства о пенсии / Приказ НКО ССР №

Командир части

М а й ор      подпись

Печать Войсковая часть Полевая Почта 1894

4.130 –

*The notes of my grandfather before passing at war*

*My mum's parents in Leningrad*

*My parents' wedding day*

*My parents*

*My mum*

*My parents and me*

*Saving my grandma Valentina's tomatoes in cold May*

# 8

## FIRST FLIGHT

**W**ho we become and how we communicate as adults stem from our early environment. We learn from the way the grown-ups around us behave, and that becomes our belief system. We try to test these beliefs, of course, when we become teenagers. Then later, in adulthood, we strongly regret not believing what our parents taught us in the first place!

It's quite normal for adolescents to challenge their parents. Then in the years between our teens and our 30s, we don't give much thought to questions like *Who am I? Where do I come from? Where am I going?* because we are preoccupied with searching for our life partners, raising a family and following our careers. But eventually, we reach a point where we must seek answers to these three key questions in order to develop as individuals.

The memories of positive and negative experiences remain with you forever and are triggered when you take part in a similar activity. My first experience of flying, when I was four years old, is a classic example. I remember the green leaves on the trees in Moscow were starting to turn brown, and autumn was not far away. My parents had planned a holiday, which was not only going to be my first experience of flying but also my first visit to the seaside.

We were going to Georgia, then part of the Soviet Union, where Mum and Dad liked to spend their vacations every year. It's a fantastic country with beautiful scenery and wonderful, hospitable people. When I woke up, the sun was shining, and I saw the suitcases had already been packed. I couldn't contain my excitement. I'd never even seen a plane close-up before, only in the sky.

We packed our luggage into a taxi and set off on the long drive to the airport. At the airport, we went to the café where the tables were covered in fresh, white, ironed cloths. My dad asked if I wanted something to eat or drink, and I said tomato juice because it's something I've always loved. He told me to be careful to hold the glass in my hand and not to spill anything on the white cloth. I heard what he said, but I didn't do as I was told, and when the tomato juice arrived, I started messing about with the glass.

Inevitably, it tipped over, and I remember the juice running towards my dad like a river of blood. It was impossible to clean up the mess with a serviette, and my mum and dad were highly embarrassed, while I was just annoyed I wouldn't get to taste the tomato juice! My parents had never been angry with me before, but they said that if you are in a public place, you must behave the way you are told. That was rule number one, and to this day, I always behave myself in public – eating properly, not arguing and so on. It's part of that childhood belief system.

As the time of our flight approached, I was jumping around asking everyone when we would be taking off. I remember walking up lots of steps and ending up inside the plane. The smell was amazing – I still remember it – something between clean air, caramel and very nice, flowery perfume – and there were spotlessly clean, white headrests on the seats.

Next to my seat, there was a little table where I was told I could draw if I wanted to, but I didn't want to draw. I just wanted to take it all in. The stewardess, with her bright red lipstick, smiled at us and asked if we needed anything. In those days, they used to give passengers lemonade and sweets before the flight. The last thing I remember is drinking the lemonade!

Sometime later, I woke up on a bed, with my mum trying to undress me. I asked her what she was doing and why we weren't on the plane. It turned out that, somehow, I had managed to sleep through the whole flight. Since then, every experience I have of a plane reminds me of that holiday. I love flying. Nothing is more exciting. I could fly every day and never tire of it. My excitement before a plane journey is so strong that I can't sleep the night before. Yet the moment I put away my hand luggage and take my seat, I am out like a light!

I've been flying with a lot of different companions – two husbands, my latest boyfriend, my son – and none of them could believe how quickly this happened. I try to stay awake by reading a book or having a chat, but nothing works. It's only when I'm on a flight of six or seven hours or more that I will sometimes wake up to have something to eat or stretch my legs. Most of the time, I have no recollection of the flight at all!

My love of flying is doubtless linked to my love of visiting different countries and learning something new at every destination.

# 9

## MY DNA JOURNEY

Last year for my birthday I was given a DNA kit. I hesitated about sending off my sample to start with because I saw myself as a child of the universe who didn't belong anywhere. But, at the same time, I have always been curious about the origin of my looks and my unusual surname so I decided to take the plunge.

It's a big world, and with travel, we don't just learn about other cultures, but also about ourselves. Putting ourselves in strange and unfamiliar places is all part of growing up. Even learning a little bit of another language is good because it shows respect to others.

My mum taught German and knew Spanish quite well because some of her students came from Cuba and other Spanish-speaking countries. I was always aware of this. Because of my father's job, we often entertained people of different nationalities and religions too. Sometimes we would have Jews and Muslims sitting at the same table, and we never differentiated. I grew up with that in mind.

Anyway, two months after sending off my DNA sample, I got the results and, to my shock, found I identified with a lot of different cultures – Finnish, Swedish, Baltic, part of Byzantia (which is in Turkey now). In all, 1,520 people were my distant cousins. When I saw that one distant cousin had the name Katherine Storina on her family tree, goose bumps ran down my back.

The lady was already in her 80s, and I managed to contact her. She said Katherine Storina was an immigrant who had arrived in New York from one of the Baltic States, but that the surname had disappeared when she married. After that, I learned of more and more cousins through my DNA, and it made me realise how our world is not as big as we think. When we travel, it's quite possibly to places where our ancestors lived. We are going back to our roots. Maybe that's why some places mean more to us than others.

My favourite continent is Europe, and I think of myself as a European woman. I had the chance to go to New Zealand but couldn't move so far away. I enjoyed my trips to Israel and Spain and am very fond of Turkey, with its fascinating history of Byzantia and the Orthodox church, and also countries in the Middle East.

But I have a particular love for Barbados because the sea there is unbelievable and the people are amazing. I first went there in 1998 and have returned 10 times since. The history of the slave trade upsets me profoundly: the idea of people being dragged from their homes, put on slave ships and treated badly is simply horrific to me. It was no wonder they designed their own language of Bajan and their own distinct culture, because everything we know of freedom was taken away from them.

The island's history museum illustrates just what happens when we ignore our DNA and forget we have no right to put another in slavery and make money out of it. The remarkable thing is that, while all this happened comparatively recently, Barbadians are always positive and cheerful.

Once, we hired an open-topped car, and all of a sudden, traffic was stopped for no reason. We waited patiently, being familiar with traffic jams in the UK, then decided to check what was causing the delay. It turned out to be a bus, with passengers getting on and off while the bus driver was eating his lunch! We asked him why he'd stopped for half an hour, and he said, 'If I don't take my lunch at the right time, my wife would be very cross!' and the whole bus agreed with him that lunch must be eaten at the right time and never in a hurry.

We were laughing and thinking, *Try telling them that in the UK!* because everything is done in such a rush, you can't remember what you had for breakfast. In contrast, these people have rules passed on from generation to generation and have respect for someone who prepares food for them. So, you sit and enjoy what was given.

As we travelled further around the island, we saw fruit hanging from a mango tree. We tried to hit a mango down to the ground like three crazy people, and my son, like a little monkey, tried to climb the tree. From nowhere, an old native man approached with a smile on his face. I told Nick to get down because the tree belonged to this man. But to our amazement, the old man took off his hat and wished us the best of health and happiness and asked us if we'd like some mangoes. He was hurrying to tell us that if we ate them straight from the tree, they might give us a stomach upset because they were not ripe. He invited us to his house, where he said he had ripe mangoes in the garden.

We didn't know what to expect. We were mesmerised. His wooden house was very clean but simple. He gave us a full pack of mangoes. When we drove back, we all became sad thinking of that man's roots in Africa and the fact that his ancestors were slaves. Yet his spirit was so strong and kind that he would give white people a present from his garden.

We offered to pay for the mangoes, but he was so cross. 'It's not mine. It's a gift from God, and all I do is share that with you,' he said. From that day, every time I visit Barbados, I remember his smiling face, and I hope he is still healthy and happy. Taking that DNA test made me believe that liking that man was perhaps because a tiny part of me belonged to his DNA and Barbados.

# 10

## SIGNPOST TO A NEW CAREER

I'm often asked why I chose a career in audiology. There are actually two very different reasons.

When I was young, I wanted to be a doctor, but my mum said, 'There are no doctors in our family'. Being an obedient child, that was that. But the desire to study medicine must have stayed in the back of my mind, and when I looked into the science of audiology later in life, it seemed the next best thing.

There was, however, another really strong reason related to my experiences as a young mum, which may sound a bit crazy! My son, Nicolai, was born in August 1986, in the middle of a really hot summer. When I took him home from hospital, I was panicking because, being a young mum, it all seemed such a big responsibility.

It's something I had started experiencing in pregnancy too. We're all different, of course, but when you become pregnant at a young age, it's a strange experience, something I couldn't imagine. It's as if it's not your body anymore, like you have become the 'host' to some alien inside you!

Perhaps we all approach these responsibilities in a different way, based on how we were brought up. But when I became pregnant, I promised that little person inside me that I would do my best to protect him until he reached adulthood. I calculated I would still be quite young when my baby reached 18 years of age, and after that, I would focus on my own life – and that is exactly what happened.

I became a very strong mother, sometimes a bit controlling I suppose, but whatever I did it was with the best intentions. I always told my son I didn't ask him to come into my life. Knowing how the universe works, sometimes you are not asking for certain things to happen, but as vibrational beings, we attract another soul to come to us – and perhaps this was the case with him.

In the first few months of the pregnancy, I didn't experience morning sickness or any other symptoms. I was told by my mum that if you're pregnant, you will feel sick when you brush your teeth, but I didn't! I was really worried about what was happening to me.

I led a very active life, and when my husband came back from a month away on officer training, he remarked about the fact I'd put on weight. For a young woman, that's not a very nice thing to hear, and we had a massive argument. But when I went shopping, I realised he was right because I couldn't get into clothes my normal size.

My grandmother told me to see the doctor because I might be suffering from some kind of illness. No one asked if was pregnant, but I was eating a lot of sweets when I had never had a sweet tooth. I also had a desire for beer, which was ridiculous because I had never drunk it before, but all of a sudden, when I smelt beer as I was passing shops or when someone was opening a bottle, I had this overwhelming urge to drink it.

Anyway, I went to the doctor, and she told me I was pregnant. I was really shocked. She asked if I was married, and I said, 'Yes, of course.' So she said, 'Why are you so surprised?' I told her I'd never had morning sickness, and she laughed and said not everyone does.

When I went home and told my husband, he was shocked too and said, 'Oh my God, what are we going to do?' It seemed a strange reaction and not very supportive, but we were both very young. In the movies, men are over the moon when they find out their wives are pregnant, whereas he was scared to even kiss me, as if it was a disease and he had to keep his distance in case he caught it. That's how it felt anyway.

Throughout my pregnancy, I was determined to stay healthy, avoiding alcohol, sweets, anything that would 'pollute' my body. I don't know where I learned that, probably just a survival instinct, and when you are 20, you don't want your body to become like a sack of potatoes – you want to stay slim.

I decided to do as much swimming and walking as I could.

At that time, we lived in a 12th floor apartment. You may think I was crazy – I think that now too – but for months, I never took the lift. But, as I became heavier, those stairs became harder and harder to climb. That was really what made me start learning about the body and physiology from keep-fit books I borrowed from the library, in days before you could read about it on the internet.

I also developed this strange fear that my child might be born deaf. I don't even know where that came from. I had never known any deaf people in my life. But I started reading medical books that mentioned this possibility, and it really scared me. Looking back, maybe I was afraid my child would be different from others and an embarrassment, because it's a natural survival extinct to want to fit in with those around you.

Luckily, my baby was delivered OK, but the first thing I asked was if he was deaf. The doctor looked at me as if I was nuts and said, 'What's the matter with you? You should be asking different questions' – and that thought is still with me. In the weeks after that, I kept trying to test his hearing by clapping my hands to see if he looked towards the sound.

I became even more convinced there was a problem when the dog barked and he didn't respond. At that time, we had a dog called Tosha, who would bark hysterically if someone knocked the door or the phone rang, and my child would sleep through it.

I remember the nurse visiting and saying she was very pleased with how the baby was developing, with his weight and everything else, and I started crying and said I was worried he was deaf and explained about the dog. She started laughing at me and said, 'Did you have the dog when you were pregnant?' and I said, 'Yes,' she said, 'Well, the dog was barking then, and your child was developing his hearing a long time before he came out into the world!'

So, I went in search of more books about hearing and how it works, not realising that nearly 20 years later, I would end up studying for a degree in audiology at Swansea University. I think my experience shows that, even though you may not be aware of it at the time, fear can be your biggest motivational force, bringing you to the place where you need to be.

Nothing in our life just materialises there and then. Everything is processed, and the good and bad happen for a reason. In 2004, feeling sick to my stomach from the prospect of studying in a foreign language in my mid-30s with a big mortgage to pay and my husband in poor health, I started my journey into audiology at Swansea University. There wasn't any way back for me then.

If we look at our fears with an open mind, they can become a positive thing, and as in my case, they might even lead to a new career!

# 11

## CAR CRASH 'MIRACLE'

Sometimes, a totally unexpected event changes our lives forever. For me, a significant turning point came in April 1990, when we were travelling from Germany to Moscow to pay a surprise visit to my parents at Easter. We had moved to Germany in 1986, when Nic was three. It was our first car, and we were very excited. We were young, successful, enjoying our new life in a different country, doing well financially, quite adventurous, had a beautiful little boy and had just got a German poodle with a good pedigree – everything in life was good.

I was spending a lot of time with Nicolai, our sensitive little boy, because I was not working. I was, however, still studying for my choreography degree in Moscow, which meant travelling back and forth by train, with my son and our new puppy now as extra 'baggage'! My husband was very good and made sure we always travelled in comfort and were well looked after, and we'd be met in Moscow by my parents or in-laws.

Having our own car was exciting. We'd been married five years, and everyone said we were doing very well. Maybe things were all happening too fast for our age, maybe not. Either way, we were feeling proud of ourselves and wanted to surprise our families.

My husband was still a young man with very little experience of driving. On that fateful weekend, we packed our things into the car and set off, with our new and fashionable Japanese tape recorder deliberately displayed on the back seat! By the time we reached Brest, which was then on the Soviet Union border with Poland but is now in Belarus, he was getting tired, and we probably should have stopped for a break, but we wanted to push on.

It was a lovely, clear road first thing in the morning, and we were feeling relaxed. Then suddenly, without any warning, two of our tyres burst, and our car – and our whole world – turned upside down. Maybe my husband had put too much pressure in those tyres. Who knows? He didn't have much of an idea about car maintenance!

I vividly remember, as the car was turning over and over, saying, 'God help us. God help us. God help my son,' and telling them not to be frightened. It was as if everything was happening in slow motion. I couldn't get out because I was pinned in by my seatbelt, and the car had ended up on its roof. I could only move my hand. My husband was unconscious, and I couldn't see the dog, but worst of all, I couldn't see my beloved little boy.

I tried to reach into the back seat, but I couldn't feel him or see him. I kept repeating his name, but there was no answer. As if by magic, two strangers appeared from nowhere, broke into the car, cut my seatbelt and dragged me out through the windscreen As I was freed, I looked around and asked where we were because, although I could see the road sign pointing to where we were heading, we seemed to be facing in the opposite direction.

We must have landed in the middle of the motorway, which was fortunately quiet at the time. I suddenly realised, to my horror, that I couldn't see Nick anywhere. Then, as I turned around, I saw a truck coming down the road in the opposite direction swerving from side to side, as if the driver was trying to apply the brakes at high speed. My first thought was that he must be drunk.

I started screaming for my son, but there was still no sign of him. Then I suddenly saw him on the opposite carriageway, the side where we had crashed, and realised the truck was heading straight towards him and that the driver was trying frantically not to hit him. I don't understand it to this day, but the speed I found to snatch that little boy out of danger was incredible. In bare feet, I covered the distance in such a short time it was as if I had a propeller attached to my back.

The truck driver must have been terrified, not just about hitting one person but now two. He missed us by such a small margin that I literally felt the wind from the lorry's brakes on my back. My current boyfriend, who has a truck company, always says you should stay at a safe distance from trucks because the force of gravity makes it impossible for them to brake quickly.

When the truck eventually stopped, it had jack-knifed and was blocking the whole of the motorway. The poor driver came running up using swear words I had never heard in my life before. I couldn't tell if he was praising what I'd done or criticising me for the risk I'd taken!

When I grabbed my son, my first reaction was to check him all over for cuts and bruises, but he didn't have a scratch on him. Why and how he had turned up on the other side of the road, with no shoes on, not even crying, just standing there looking at me, I still don't know or understand. If miracles exist, then this was indeed a miracle.

Whatever you call God in a religious or spiritual way, it's a power that is bigger than us and keeps us safe – and realising this profoundly affected me. It didn't seem possible that my little boy had survived unscathed. When I asked him, 'How on earth did you turn up over here?' his answer was, 'Mum don't shake me. You're scaring me. It was an angel that brought me here.'

Today, it's fashionable to take an interest in spirituality, and it's perfectly acceptable to talk about angels. But at that time, when we were just in our 20s, we didn't discuss something like that at all. Yet my son was convinced he was saved by an angel. Afterwards, I asked him again and again to explain, but he just said, 'Mum, an angel is an angel.

Why are you asking?' as if he knew but couldn't put it into words.

Years later, when he went to school, some of his paintings were shown in an exhibition. One was of an angel, and another was of St Nicholas crossing the sea in a boat. They seemed strange subjects for him to draw, but his teacher said he was a very deep child and could see things other children did not.

My husband nearly died in that accident, and it shook both of us to the core. He is still alive now and is a very successful man, although he had survived by the skin of his teeth. The affect on me was that it very strongly triggered my understanding of God or 'energy'.

When my son grew up, he didn't talk about any of this, but I know deep inside him, it's still there. When he decided to join the British army and served in Afghanistan, although I was terrified, I knew he would be OK. There was no chance that the little boy who I snatched from the path of that lorry would go to a different country and be pushed through the horror of any war and have his life taken away. I know he is here for a greater reason, even if I don't know what this reason is, and maybe he doesn't either.

He is now 35 years old, still a comparatively young man, but that understanding that he is protected has always been with me, and I know that wherever he is in the world, he will always be safe because of that miracle. I am convinced that in this life, miracles happen every day. We may only be aware of the dramatic ones, but there are countless small miracles too.

Our very existence to me is a miracle, and the Earth is a big ship moving in an ever-expanding universe. From that crash, I discovered that there is an energy greater than ourselves. It went a long way to explain the answers I was seeking years later to who I am, where I come from and where I am going.

# 12

## RESCUE MISSION

I phoned my mother in Moscow from the local police was still shaking from the shock of the crash when I station. I remember telling her Nick and I were OK so not to worry, but my husband was badly injured and might die. My dear mother was silent at first, then, trying to stay calm for me, she whispered, 'Don't worry. I will sort something out.' And I knew then that she would.

When I told her where we were after the car crash, which was about 1,000 kilometres (more than 620 miles) from Moscow, to my amazement, it wasn't a big problem for her to find the right people to willingly help her daughter. The rescue team was quickly dispatched to take care of us, including a kind lady called Alla, whose mother just happened to be my mum's friend and who lived next door to her and her husband, Victor.

While my husband was lying in the hospital with a broken neck, these wonderful people provided accommodation for us as well as mental, physical and emotional support for me (then only 24 years old), my little boy and our dog. Many years later, in 2020, I was stuck in the UK during the COVID pandemic, so their daughter Nelly, who is now more than just a special friend, was looking after my mum when she was on her death bed.

On my mum's arrival, another rescue mission was organised almost immediately – to find our dog, Stevie. There was still no sign of our puppy, who had escaped during the car accident, and we were searching all around the area for days but now with Mum and my little boy in charge.

Victor said we should go back to the crashed car because we needed to collect evidence and recover the car key. To our surprise, we found a half-eaten baked potato on the back seat and someone moving in the bush. The joy we all felt was unbelievable. The little creature was clearly devoted to us and had waited patiently for us for the entire week, feeding on the scraps of food that he found in the wrecked car. He gave us the pleasure of his company for many years until he eventually died of old age. Not surprisingly, he developed a strong bond with my mum.

That summer, I was due to complete my first degree at MGIK – Moscow State University of Culture and Arts. But I didn't feel like finishing it and wanted to take a year off because I was still feeling tired and emotionally drawn. Thankfully, my mum had other ideas, telling me, 'There are no quitters in this family!' With her encouragement to 'focus and move forward,' I duly completed my degree two months later in June 1990.

After that, we returned to Germany, which I regarded as home, and where we had so many good times and lots of friends. In fact, I have always been happier living outside my homeland. I realised that I was not like my parents, who were always happy to return to Moscow after travelling.

My husband, however, was keen to return to Russia, so we said our goodbyes. I cried in the car for the whole journey, feeling instinctively that it was the wrong decision.

# 13

## FROM DARKNESS INTO LIGHT

We were greeted in Moscow with dirty streets, empty shops and angry people with revolution in their hearts. I started working as head of choreography at a cultural school for children. It wasn't long before tanks and barricades, gunfire and other terrifying symbols of war become a normal feature of life. It was the end of 1993.

If something bad happens to you directly – and we have all been in that situation – you take it personally and feel you are a victim. And that's exactly how I felt. Whoever did this to you is your enemy. You don't see that there is a reason for everything. Once you realise that there is more to life than what is immediately in front of you, things change.

During this time, I read a book that my mother had kept for me, which said, 'I only ask to have a love in my heart . . . the rest in life I can make it myself'. I have changed that to 'with God in my heart, all things are possible'. Love is not given because you are good or bad. Love already exists when you are born. That is where my journey started.

I was brought up following the philosophy that you do not kill, do not cheat, do not steal, etc. But that's not only a religious thing of course– it's the right thing to do. Otherwise, there would be anarchy. And once more, since 1917, my country had become a homeland of anarchy due to the political crisis known as Black October. Sitting without lights and hearing tanks moving on the street made me strongly believe that war isn't the solution.

After that year, people started going to church again, standing close to each other and praying, feeling that we were once again facing a life or death situation. My grandparents, who remembered the war so clearly, and my parents, who had been just babies then, became strong ambassadors for negotiations.

You can believe in things or not. People can believe in gravity or not, but the law of the universe is still that gravity exists. You can believe in God or not – it doesn't make any difference. Again, what is a belief? There are so many concepts of it. It's like in a war. Each side believes they are right!

I believe we are all connected by the same energy– it's not negotiable. You can believe in that energy or not– it doesn't change anything. If we choose to believe in that energy, you can channel it for good.

At New Year 1994, there were unforgettable celebrations that gave people hope that life would return to normal. Once more, it happened – by overcoming an obstacle, I had taken another step on my soul journey.

# 14

## DAFFODILS AND DRAGONS

I happen to be the national flower of my adopted country love daffodils, so it's maybe appropriate that they just of Wales. I think of them as little suns trying to shine their light towards us after a long winter, giving us hope that summer is on its way. Here in Wales, they bloom in time for St David's Day on 1ˢᵗ March, whereas in my homeland of Russia, they don't put in an appearance until early May, after the long and cold winter months.

In 1996, my grandparents Feodor and Valentina were gone, and my parents had got divorced just after they had started building a large house on the lake outside the city. My dad unexpectedly became ill with a stroke, and my mum had problems driving back and forth to work due to her failing eyesight.

My husband came up with idea of leaving me and our boy and moving forward in his life with another lady who had become his business partner. I had finished my job at choreography school to help my son settle into his new school. That year, the world I knew simply slammed the door in my face, taking away my family, my love and my sense of belonging.

After one of many sleepless nights, I went to see my grandma Galina. She took a long look at me, then asked me if I could visit my grandparents' grave and read them a letter she had written, as she was afraid of not being able to do it herself. She kindly offered to look after my boy so that I could spend some time alone to reflect on my life. She told me that life would take care of things without me trying to fix it.

Her letter to my grandparents was full of appreciation for the deep friendship the three of them had developed. And then she asked them to give me a sign for a new direction. I was sitting next to two gravestones, listening to a church bell somewhere in the distance, when two white doves magically appeared and landed on the pine tree next to my grandparents' grave.

Slowly walking back, I went into the church. When I started to pray, I didn't know what to ask. On my way out, a priest gave me an icon of St Nicholas and said he was the protector of those who travel far from their homeland. Of course it didn't make any sense to me then, as I had no plans to travel.

After that day, my self-preservation instinct kicked in, and later that month, I channelled all my resources into starting to rebuild my life. I rented a big, open place and began letting the small units to people selling everything from clothing to perfume, toys and TVs, anything that new business owners in Russia could bring from China. Along the way, I made new friends.

One of my new tenants told me that she was going to study for a degree in Canada and was taking her little girl with her. I became very interested in that idea and started searching on my first computer for more information. During my search, I read about the Hagia Sophia of Constantinople, the largest Eastern Orthodox Church of the Byzantine Empire, now the Sophia Grand Mosque in Istanbul. I thought that a holiday in Istanbul would be great with two of my new friends.

But the night before the flight, I started worrying about leaving my son with his dad and his new woman for a week. My mind must have been playing tricks with me because I had a strange dream. I was walking in the snow in Red Square, and there was no one around. Then I heard the waves of the sea and could see a row of daffodils leading me towards a dragon.

In the morning, I called one of my travel companions to say I was cancelling my break and would be back at work that day, only to hear that another friend had become ill. Feeling terrible for letting my new friend down, as it wouldn't be possible for her to travel alone, I called a taxi to take me to the airport.

On our arrival in Istanbul, I couldn't find my suitcase and went to report it missing. As I approached the desk, I saw that a guy wearing a bright red rugby shirt with a daffodil on the front pocket and the shape of a dragon on the back was holding my luggage. He explained that my suitcase must have come to his baggage carousel by mistake because the flights from Moscow and London had arrived at the same time.

That was how I met my second husband, David. He was half Welsh and half German and was the reason why I eventually came to Wales. We were married for 14 years, sharing our love for animals, travel and history. He died from a genetic heart condition in 2012.

# 15

## PUSHING FORWARD

My constant companion today is my little Pomeranian, Coco. She is beautiful, and of course I spoil her. I buy her lovely food and enjoy her company. People ask me if she suffers from separation anxiety when I go to work and I say, 'No, but I do!' Her company is magical, and I always think I must have done something good in my life for me to be sent this gorgeous creature. She constantly makes me smile and completes my life with her unconditional love.

The other day, I was feeding her some dried organic chicken, and it occurred to me that not that long ago, our grandparents couldn't afford chicken to feed themselves. It made me think how much our grandparents in Russia and Wales had sacrificed for our generation and how little we really understand the hardships they faced.

We appreciate another person's problems when we have had the same experiences, but nowadays, compared to the lives of our predecessors, we all have a good life. In the generations born after the war, it has always been possible to find success if you have a good brain and the motivation. There is nothing stopping you. Sometimes, we have better times than others, but at least we always have food on the table.

When I came to Wales, I discovered how hard they used to work in the coal mines and steel industry to make Britain great, how little they had and what a strong community they had built because of it.

I used to work in the NHS, and driving to home visits, I remember how lovely and welcoming people were. They had never met a Russian before, but they always invited me in for a cup of tea and a biscuit. It was overwhelming. I would see photographs there of the generations before them who worked in the dark in the mines to bring in a few pounds to provide for the family. I learned that in Wales, some people back then didn't even have an indoor toilet, which amazed me.

As I was feeding Coco her organic chicken, my thoughts turned to the people both here in Wales and in Russia who did so much for us – looking after us when we were children, giving us everything we needed in order for our generation to have a better life. But it makes me sad to find that in the UK, there are still so many children whose parents are unable to look after them.

I can't understand how that is possible when food from the supermarkets is thrown away in the rubbish bins and some children only have proper meals at school. Working in a Newport hospital, I have learned that some families have been unemployed for two generations and are claiming money off the state, that they can't afford food for their children yet can smoke and drink alcohol.

At the same time, there are so many amazing people in Wales! I see them every day in my clinic. They are working hard, making Wales a safe and nice place to call home, some even fostering children. I know so many people who are working even in their 70s, serving the community through dedication to voluntary work, church or children and also a wonderful generation of people who are proudly retired but support their community with the wisdom that they gained through their life. Wales has become my second home!

Those people are inspiring me to create a charity trust designed to provide every foster child with free ear health. I hope that giving something to children in my adopted and safe home of Wales will help me to make positive changes, leaving my DNA legacy for future generations. When I set off from Moscow on my journey into the unknown all those years ago, clutching my little boy's hand, I was fearful of what lay ahead.

I wished so much that my wonderful grandparents – the Three Musketeers – were there to wave me on to a new phase of my life, just as they had been on my first day at school. But I appreciate now that they WERE there in spirit, pushing me gently forwards with the words that have rung in my ears since I was little: 'Come on, go, go . . .'

I am so glad I made that journey from Russia to Wales – with love.

StoryTerrace

CPSIA information can be obtained
at www.ICGtesting.com
Printed in the USA
BVHW012119030223
657824BV00015B/1295

9 781982 286538